This book contains the plans and goals of:

_____

_____

_____

PLANNER

Goal:

_____

Set yourself a goal for this year.

Step: _____ Deadline: _____

Step: _____ Deadline: _____

Step: _____ Deadline: _____

Step: _____ Deadline: _____

Step: _____ Deadline: _____

Step: _____ Deadline: _____

Step: _____ Deadline: _____

Step: _____ Deadline: _____

Step: _____ Deadline: _____

Step: _____ Deadline: _____

Step: _____ Deadline: _____

Step: _____ Deadline: _____

Step: _____ Deadline: _____

Step: _____ Deadline: _____

Goal:

_____

Set yourself a goal for this year.

Step: _____ Deadline: _____

Step: _____ Deadline: _____

Step: _____ Deadline: _____

Step: _____ Deadline: _____

Step: _____ Deadline: _____

Step: _____ Deadline: _____

Step: _____ Deadline: _____

Step: _____ Deadline: _____

Step: _____ Deadline: _____

Step: _____ Deadline: _____

Step: _____ Deadline: _____

Step: _____ Deadline: _____

Step: _____ Deadline: _____

Step: _____ Deadline: _____

Goal:

_____

Set yourself a goal for this year.

Step: _____ Deadline: _____

Step: _____ Deadline: _____

Step: _____ Deadline: _____

Step: _____ Deadline: _____

Step: _____ Deadline: _____

Step: _____ Deadline: _____

Step: _____ Deadline: _____

Step: _____ Deadline: _____

Step: _____ Deadline: _____

Step: _____ Deadline: _____

Step: _____ Deadline: _____

Step: _____ Deadline: _____

Step: _____ Deadline: _____

Step: _____ Deadline: _____

Goal:

_____

Set yourself a goal for this year.

Step: _____ Deadline: _____

Step: _____ Deadline: _____

Step: _____ Deadline: _____

Step: _____ Deadline: _____

Step: _____ Deadline: _____

Step: _____ Deadline: _____

Step: _____ Deadline: _____

Step: _____ Deadline: _____

Step: _____ Deadline: _____

Step: _____ Deadline: _____

Step: _____ Deadline: _____

Step: _____ Deadline: _____

Step: _____ Deadline: _____

Step: _____ Deadline: _____

Goal:

_____

Set yourself a goal for this year.

Step: _____ Deadline: _____

Step: _____ Deadline: _____

Step: _____ Deadline: _____

Step: _____ Deadline: _____

Step: _____ Deadline: _____

Step: _____ Deadline: _____

Step: _____ Deadline: _____

Step: _____ Deadline: _____

Step: _____ Deadline: _____

Step: _____ Deadline: _____

Step: _____ Deadline: _____

Step: _____ Deadline: _____

Step: _____ Deadline: _____

Step: _____ Deadline: _____

Goal:

_____

Set yourself a goal for this year.

Step: _____ Deadline: _____

Step: _____ Deadline: _____

Step: _____ Deadline: _____

Step: _____ Deadline: _____

Step: _____ Deadline: _____

Step: _____ Deadline: _____

Step: _____ Deadline: _____

Step: _____ Deadline: _____

Step: _____ Deadline: _____

Step: _____ Deadline: _____

Step: _____ Deadline: _____

Step: _____ Deadline: _____

Step: _____ Deadline: _____

Step: _____ Deadline: _____

Month of _____

Sunday	Monday	Tuesday	Wednesday

Thursday	Friday	Saturday	Goals:

Month of _____

Sunday	Monday	Tuesday	Wednesday

Thursday	Friday	Saturday	Goals:

Month of _____

Sunday	Monday	Tuesday	Wednesday

Thursday	Friday	Saturday	Goals:

Month of _____

Sunday	Monday	Tuesday	Wednesday

Thursday	Friday	Saturday	Goals:

Month of _____

Sunday	Monday	Tuesday	Wednesday

Thursday	Friday	Saturday	Goals:

Month of _____

Sunday	Monday	Tuesday	Wednesday

Thursday	Friday	Saturday	Goals:

Month of _____

Sunday	Monday	Tuesday	Wednesday

Thursday	Friday	Saturday	Goals:

Month of _____

Sunday	Monday	Tuesday	Wednesday

Thursday	Friday	Saturday	Goals:

Month of _____

Sunday	Monday	Tuesday	Wednesday

Thursday	Friday	Saturday	Goals:

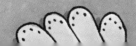

Month of _____

Sunday	Monday	Tuesday	Wednesday

Thursday	Friday	Saturday	Goals:

Month of _____

Sunday	Monday	Tuesday	Wednesday

Thursday	Friday	Saturday	Goals:

Month of _____

Sunday	Monday	Tuesday	Wednesday

Thursday	Friday	Saturday	Goals:

Week of _____

Goals for the week:

Sunday	
Monday	
Tuesday	
Wednesday	

Thursday	
Friday	
Saturday	

Things to do:

Notes:

Week of _____

Goals for the week:

Sunday	
Monday	
Tuesday	
Wednesday	

Thursday

Friday

Saturday

Things to do:

Notes:

Week of _____

Goals for the week:

Sunday

Monday

Tuesday

Wednesday

Thursday

Friday

Saturday

Things to do:

Notes:

Week of _____

Goals for the week:

Sunday	
Monday	
Tuesday	
Wednesday	

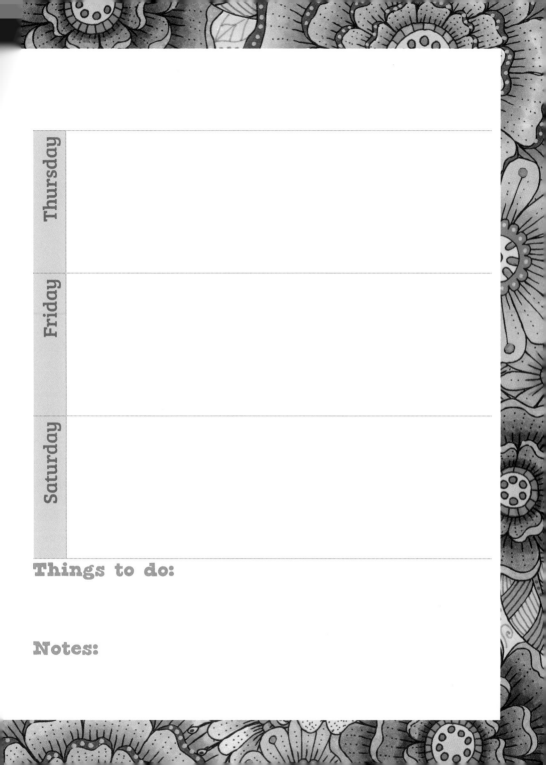

Thursday

Friday

Saturday

Things to do:

Notes:

Week of _____

Goals for the week:

Sunday	
Monday	
Tuesday	
Wednesday	

Thursday

Friday

Saturday

Things to do:

Notes:

Week of _____

Goals for the week:

Sunday

Monday

Tuesday

Wednesday

Thursday

Friday

Saturday

Things to do:

Notes:

Week of _____

Goals for the week:

Sunday	
Monday	
Tuesday	
Wednesday	

Thursday	
Friday	
Saturday	

Things to do:

Notes:

Week of _____

Goals for the week:

Sunday	
Monday	
Tuesday	
Wednesday	

Thursday

Friday

Saturday

Things to do:

Notes:

Week of _____

Goals for the week:

Sunday	
Monday	
Tuesday	
Wednesday	

Thursday

Friday

Saturday

Things to do:

Notes:

Week of _____

Goals for the week:

Sunday	
Monday	
Tuesday	
Wednesday	

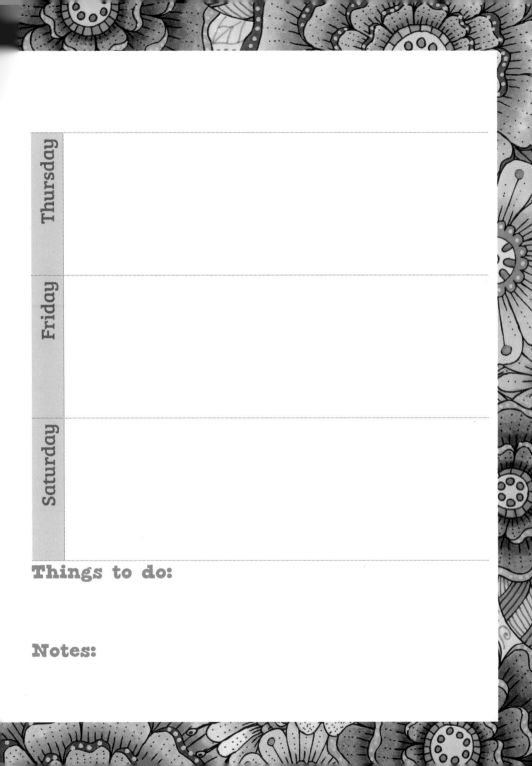

Thursday

Friday

Saturday

Things to do:

Notes:

Week of _____

Goals for the week:

Sunday	
Monday	
Tuesday	
Wednesday	

Thursday

Friday

Saturday

Things to do:

Notes:

Week of _____

Goals for the week:

Sunday	
Monday	
Tuesday	
Wednesday	

Thursday

Friday

Saturday

Things to do:

Notes:

Week of _____

Goals for the week:

Sunday	
Monday	
Tuesday	
Wednesday	

Thursday	
Friday	
Saturday	

Things to do:

Notes:

Week of _____

Goals for the week:

Sunday

Monday

Tuesday

Wednesday

Thursday	
Friday	
Saturday	

Things to do:

Notes:

Week of _____

Goals for the week:

Sunday	
Monday	
Tuesday	
Wednesday	

Thursday

Friday

Saturday

Things to do:

Notes:

Week of _____

Goals for the week:

Sunday	
Monday	
Tuesday	
Wednesday	

Thursday	
Friday	
Saturday	

Things to do:

Notes:

Week of _____

Goals for the week:

Sunday	
Monday	
Tuesday	
Wednesday	

Thursday	
Friday	
Saturday	

Things to do:

Notes:

Week of _____

Goals for the week:

Sunday

Monday

Tuesday

Wednesday

Thursday

Friday

Saturday

Things to do:

Notes:

Week of _____

Goals for the week:

Sunday

Monday

Tuesday

Wednesday

Thursday	
Friday	
Saturday	

Things to do:

Notes:

Week of _____

Goals for the week:

Sunday

Monday

Tuesday

Wednesday

Thursday

Friday

Saturday

Things to do:

Notes:

Week of _____

Goals for the week:

Sunday	
Monday	
Tuesday	
Wednesday	

Thursday	
Friday	
Saturday	

Things to do:

Notes:

Week of _____

Goals for the week:

Sunday	
Monday	
Tuesday	
Wednesday	

Thursday

Friday

Saturday

Things to do:

Notes:

Week of _____

Goals for the week:

Sunday	
Monday	
Tuesday	
Wednesday	

Thursday	
Friday	
Saturday	

Things to do:

Notes:

Week of _____

Goals for the week:

Sunday	
Monday	
Tuesday	
Wednesday	

Thursday

Friday

Saturday

Things to do:

Notes:

Week of _____

Goals for the week:

Sunday	
Monday	
Tuesday	
Wednesday	

Thursday

Friday

Saturday

Things to do:

Notes:

Week of _____

Goals for the week:

Sunday	
Monday	
Tuesday	
Wednesday	

Thursday

Friday

Saturday

Things to do:

Notes:

Week of _____

Goals for the week:

Sunday

Monday

Tuesday

Wednesday

Thursday

Friday

Saturday

Things to do:

Notes:

Week of _____

Goals for the week:

Sunday	
Monday	
Tuesday	
Wednesday	

Thursday	
Friday	
Saturday	

Things to do:

Notes:

Week of _____

Goals for the week:

Sunday	
Monday	
Tuesday	
Wednesday	

Thursday

Friday

Saturday

Things to do:

Notes:

Week of _____

Goals for the week:

Sunday	
Monday	
Tuesday	
Wednesday	

Thursday

Friday

Saturday

Things to do:

Notes:

Week of _____

Goals for the week:

Sunday	
Monday	
Tuesday	
Wednesday	

Thursday	
Friday	
Saturday	

Things to do:

Notes:

Week of ＿＿＿＿＿＿＿＿＿＿

Goals for the week:

Sunday

Monday

Tuesday

Wednesday

Thursday

Friday

Saturday

Things to do:

Notes:

Week of _____

Goals for the week:

Sunday	
Monday	
Tuesday	
Wednesday	

Thursday

Friday

Saturday

Things to do:

Notes:

Week of _____

Goals for the week:

Sunday

Monday

Tuesday

Wednesday

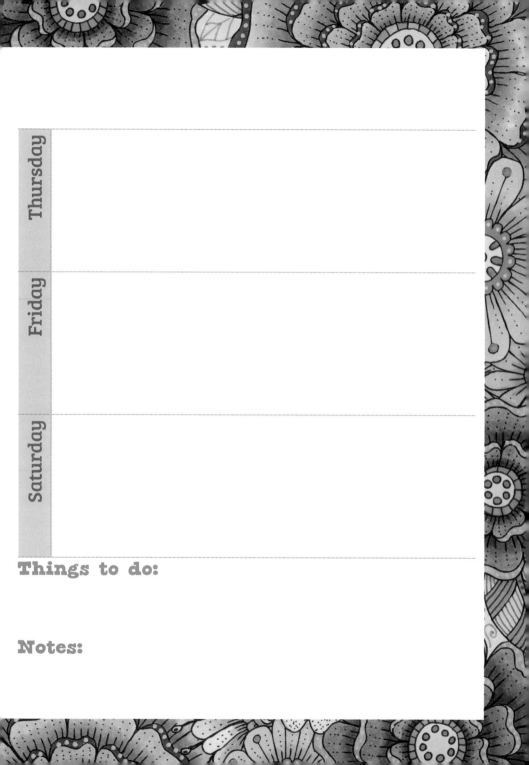

Thursday	
Friday	
Saturday	

Things to do:

Notes:

Week of _____

Goals for the week:

Sunday

Monday

Tuesday

Wednesday

Thursday

Friday

Saturday

Things to do:

Notes:

Week of _____

Goals for the week:

Sunday

Monday

Tuesday

Wednesday

Thursday

Friday

Saturday

Things to do:

Notes:

Week of _____

Goals for the week:

Sunday

Monday

Tuesday

Wednesday

Thursday

Friday

Saturday

Things to do:

Notes:

Week of _____
Goals for the week:

Sunday	
Monday	
Tuesday	
Wednesday	

Thursday

Friday

Saturday

Things to do:

Notes:

Week of _____

Goals for the week:

Sunday	
Monday	
Tuesday	
Wednesday	

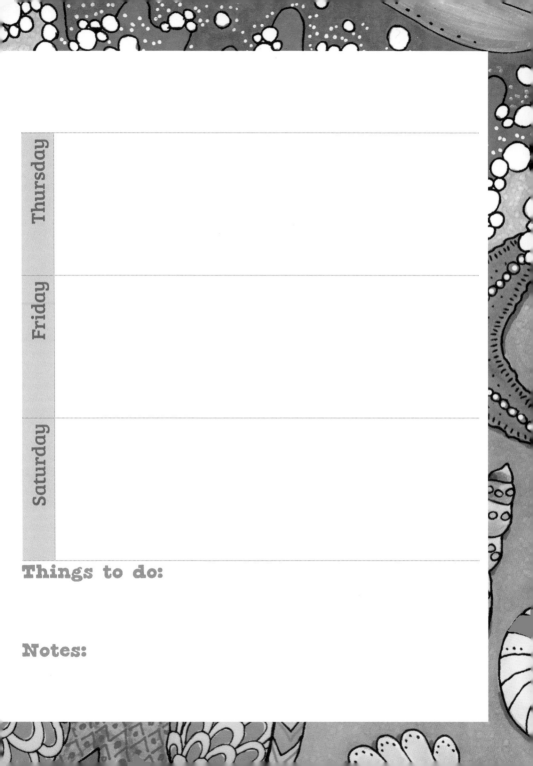

Thursday

Friday

Saturday

Things to do:

Notes:

Week of _____

Goals for the week:

Sunday	
Monday	
Tuesday	
Wednesday	

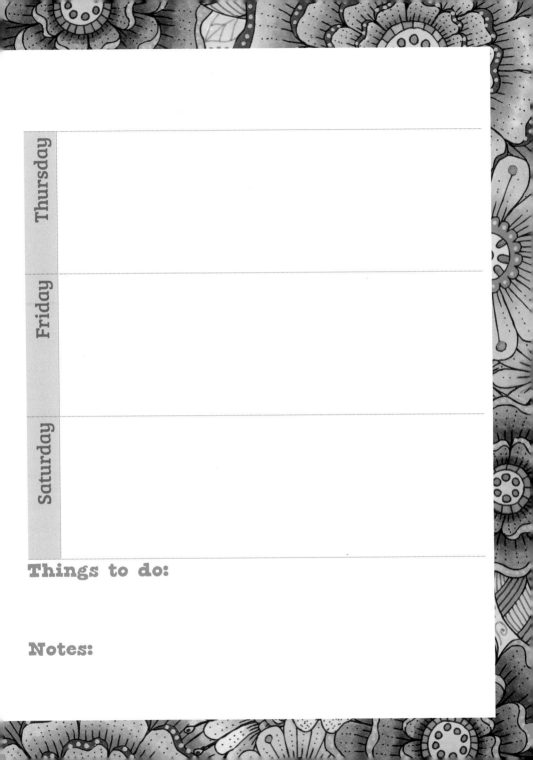

Thursday

Friday

Saturday

Things to do:

Notes:

Week of _____

Goals for the week:

Sunday	
Monday	
Tuesday	
Wednesday	

Thursday	
Friday	
Saturday	

Things to do:

Notes:

Week of _____

Goals for the week:

Sunday

Monday

Tuesday

Wednesday

Thursday	
Friday	
Saturday	

Things to do:

Notes:

Week of _____

Goals for the week:

Sunday	
Monday	
Tuesday	
Wednesday	

Thursday	
Friday	
Saturday	

Things to do:

Notes:

Week of _____

Goals for the week:

Sunday	
Monday	
Tuesday	
Wednesday	

Thursday	
Friday	
Saturday	

Things to do:

Notes:

Week of _____

Goals for the week:

Sunday	
Monday	
Tuesday	
Wednesday	

Thursday

Friday

Saturday

Things to do:

Notes:

Week of _____

Goals for the week:

Sunday	
Monday	
Tuesday	
Wednesday	

Thursday	
Friday	
Saturday	

Things to do:

Notes:

Week of _____

Goals for the week:

Sunday	
Monday	
Tuesday	
Wednesday	

Thursday	
Friday	
Saturday	

Things to do:

Notes:

Week of _____

Goals for the week:

Sunday	
Monday	
Tuesday	
Wednesday	

Thursday	
Friday	
Saturday	

Things to do:

Notes:

Week of _____

Goals for the week:

Sunday	
Monday	
Tuesday	
Wednesday	

Thursday	
Friday	
Saturday	

Things to do:

Notes:

Week of _____

Goals for the week:

Sunday	
Monday	
Tuesday	
Wednesday	

Thursday

Friday

Saturday

Things to do:

Notes:

Week of _____

Goals for the week:

Sunday

Monday

Tuesday

Wednesday

Thursday	
Friday	
Saturday	

Things to do:

Notes:

Week of _____

Goals for the week:

Sunday	
Monday	
Tuesday	
Wednesday	

Thursday	
Friday	
Saturday	

Things to do:

Notes:

Week of _____

Goals for the week:

Sunday	
Monday	
Tuesday	
Wednesday	

Thursday

Friday

Saturday

Things to do:

Notes:

About the Artist

Angelea Van Dam of Hello Angel has drawn her entire life. This New Zealand artist is a graphic designer by trade, working out of her home as a freelancer. Her color style is every color under the sun and then she likes to pile on some more! Angelea wants to be in her studio making art almost all the time. It's what makes her happy. The fact that her art inspires others makes her doubly happy and motivates her to create so much more.

Journals from Hello Angel

ISBN 978-1-64178-037-7

Fox Chapel Publishing makes every effort to use environmentally friendly paper for printing.

We are always looking for talented authors and artists. To submit an idea, please send a brief inquiry to acquisitions@foxchapelpublishing.com.

Printed in China
First printing